Que
Lindo
b o o K s
• • •

BOUNCE

a book of
paintings
&
poems

a collaboration by

Lucid Ryu
&
Alvaro Salinas Jr.

the Book

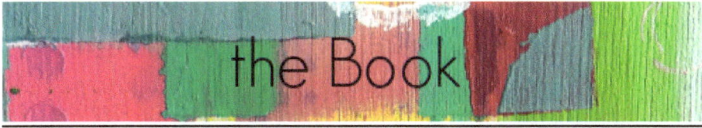

It didn't take place at a playground with a colorful ball

bouncing back and forth, but it could have.

Alvaro Salinas, Jr., and Ludid Ryu present this collaborative

book as a way to bring creative passions together

in a meaningful way.

What an opportunity to branch out and try new points of view.

The book features 10 poems alongside 10 abstract paintings.

Five poems inspired five paintings.

Five paintings inspired five poems.

Our styles evolved as a result of this collaborative project

We take this work and collaboration into our future work.

We offer our joy.

We will meet you on the playground.

Where Color Hides At Night

During the blackest hour of the night,
Julian fell into a deep sleep -

He plummeted away from the black and past the next day's light,
and into the place where Color hides at night.

Even though he read the sign "No Outside Guests,"
he found it best
to ignore it and enter the place where Color rests.

While Color dreamt of wondrous images and unique shapes it wishes
and tries,
these dreams were absorbed into Julian's open eyes.

And these dreams and visions gave him such a fright,
that he ran away from where Color hides at night.

But he remembered those colorful dreams
confined inside his head,
As he awoke, one day older,
brightly in his bed.

The Park At Night

When I close my eyes
for the night
a beautiful park
comes into sight.

       With its swings and slides
       and merry-go-round
       and lush green grass
       all around,

              with a fountain in its center
              and an oak tree by its side
              with a canopy of leaves
              over half a mile wide,

                     where under I lay
                     so my time consists
                     of doing nothing
                     but feeling the
                     fountain's mist,

              and I'll think
              and I'll decide
              that I'll never want to return
              inside,

       and I'll hide my face
       when the day starts to brighten
       and my eyes,
       I'll quickly tighten,

and I'll beg and plead
for the park to stay within sight
my park, my park,
my beautiful park -
my beautiful park at night.

The Garden

She doesn't have any toys.
She doesn't have a pretty
dress,
but she has something else
the others don't possess -

She has a garden -
where she plants and prunes
her wondrous imagination
under a gigantic moon.

She skips and sings,
between each colorful row -
laughing and dancing
with her shadow.

Her roses have grown
to be ten feet tall,
and beautiful ivy grows
over any stone wall.

Her petunias and daisies
bloom all year long.
She loves her garden
where there is never any
wrong.

.

Yet still...

some don't understand,
so they tease with nasty slurs.

I wonder if they have a garden
as wondrous as hers?

That Turtle Likes To Wear A Wig

That turtle likes to wear a wig
during the wintertime.
He bought it from his friend, the pig,
for an apple and a dime,

and when that turtle wears his wig,
he loves to paint the town -
he paints it loud - he paints it big
when the temperature goes down.

The weather can be freezing
and that turtle can be sneezing,
but he'll still think the town is prime
for stretching and squeezing -
during the wintertime,

but when the wind turns hot instead
that turtle summers on his yacht,
and his wig will not be on his head
because it is way too hot.

Pink

I like Pink
and all the pinky things
pink makes me think,
like fluffy cotton candy
and sweet pink roses,
strawberry ice cream,
and oinky pig noses.

Yes, I like pink -
Oh, I like it a lot,
but sometimes I'm told not to,
other boys say I should not.

They like blue,
and according to them,
I should like it too.
Blue footballs
and shiny blue cars,
dusty blue baseball gloves
and screeching blue guitars.

But I think -
I'll stick with pink
and let them keep blue.
Which color do you like?
Hmm?
How about you?

House Underneath The Street

Cars drive over my house
on a newly-built street,
where drivers rush to their offices
on fresh concrete.

Their horns awake me
and screechy tires end my dreams.
Huge trucks heat my tea
with their exhaust steam,

and when my house rattles
there is no need for alarm
because I can brush my teeth
without moving my arm.

With all the commotion
by the cars heading south,
I simply enter my pantry
and breakfast falls into my mouth

Yes, this place is perfect –
It is like a king's suite,
this house - my house
My wonderful house
underneath the street.

3-Leaf Clover

I'm looking for luck
in between and all over
this field filled
with clover.

While the sun shines
in a cloudless sky
and a cool autumn breeze
slithers by.

I'm searching for luck
as I lazily kneel,
and my stomach digests
my latest big meal.

Sure, I see many with three
but I want more!
I'm looking for the lucky one
with four!

So I can show my parents
and brag to my friends!
That lucky clover would guarantee me
the best weekends -

as well as days
I'm stuck in class.
No more rainy days
in the forecast.

Always first,
never last -
never slow,
always fast,

medicine that taste like candy
and never yucky -
who am I kidding? I'll never find it.
I'll never be lucky.

Clown House

The front door is as red
as the nose on his face,
and if you ever find it
it gives way to his secret place.

A place built on
his best gags and tricks.
No wood was needed
or cement mix.

He built up his walls
with top hats and red noses,
handshaking buzzers
and water-spitting roses.

He used rainbow wigs, magic wands,
and sequined bow ties,
unicycles, magic cards
and cream-filled pies.

There, he eats his meals
with wiggly, bendy spoons,
as the sun shoots rainbows
through colorful balloons.

It's his house, his home,
his precious secret place.
The only spot where he takes
the makeup off his face.

Stained-Glass Life

This stained-glass window I'm standing next to
is pouring a rainbow onto the floor -
changing its tiles and grout,
helping the floor figure out,
that it can be so much more.

Much more colorful,
much more of a delight,
with much less darkness,
and so much more bright.

So, I walk into its rainbow,
hoping to brighten my strife -
so it may change my tiles and grout,
help me figure things out,
and lead me to a new stained-glass life.

Bounce

Boy.
Ball.
Bouncing.
Off wall.

Memorizing.
Ball's leap.
Bouncing -
to sleep.

Then a stranger
comes to play.
Ball bounces
a different way.

With excitement
they announce -
a new game,
a new bounce,

a new measure,
a new ounce,
new words
to pronounce,

and just as easily
as this new bounce crept,
boy has a different life
to accept.

New bounce
catches fire,
ball bounces
higher and higher -

Faster and faster
with a new spin -
flashing colors - off and on,
morphing shapes - out and in,

confetti blasting
accompanying bands -
eventually bouncing
out of their hands -

toward the moon,
bouncing off stars,
dodging comets,
circling Mars,

influencing memoirs,
serenading guitars,
eventually theirs -
becomes ours.

Bouncing to me,
with safes and dangers,
bouncing to you
building up strangers -

shaping our bounce,
inflating our ball,
layering our bricks,
building our wall.

Boy.
Ball.
Bouncing.
Off wall.

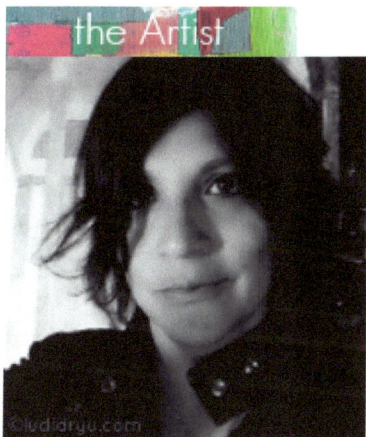
the Artist

At the heart of my artwork, I see how all my memories and experiences touch aspects of my life in various ways.

Ludid Ryu is a visual artist whose artistic expression includes painting, drawing, collaging, and journal making. Ludid is originally from Mexico City.

Ludid's imagination often pulls her back to her childhood conversations, experiences, memories and occurrences. Occasionally, Ludid lets her younger self be the guide. She enjoys going back and looking around.

An avid note-taker, Ludid is heavily inspired by variety and adding all kinds of information to her archives. Acquiring, compiling, and filing information is a way to keep her mind fresh.

Ludid lives in the Dallas area with her husband and son. As a member of the Plano Art Association, she has exhibited at several juried art shows. Publications that have featured her work include Somerset Life and Somerset Studio Gallery.

Ludid's current project, Courtyard Stories , includes an ongoing series of illustrations. The series offers a unique perspective on creating space for discoveries.

www.ludidryu.com ©2013

Alvaro lives in the Dallas area with his wife, daughter, son and cat. He is a member of the North Texas Chapter of SCBWI.

http://mmsocks.wordpress.com
©2013

Alvaro Salinas Jr. is a children's story writer who encourages children to use their imagination and creativity. Through positive, fun, thought-provoking stories and poems, Alvaro creates a world where children's ideas and creativity are allowed to run wild and experience a different view on everyday occurrences.

Alvaro Salinas Jr. writes children's poetry under the pseudonym M. M. Socks, a poet who always wears mismatched socks (M. M. Socks). The reason for wearing socks that don't match is just a visual introduction for children to embrace the idea that being different is O.K., fine or perhaps even "cool". Alvaro updates his blog of free poetry for children on a regular basis.

www.ingramcontent.com/pod-product-compliance
Lightning Source LLC
Chambersburg PA
CBHW040347060426
42445CB00029B/32

* 9 7 8 0 6 1 5 9 0 2 1 5 9 *